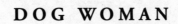

DOG WOMAN

DOG WOMAN

CHRIS ABANI

RED HEN PRESS 🐔 LOS ANGELES

Cover image "Baying" by Paula Rego.
Courtesy of Marlborough Fine Art, London.

Book design by Mark E. Cull

ISBN 1-888996-82-X
Library of Congress Catalog Card Number: 2004095866

The City of Los Angeles Cultural Affairs Department, California Arts Council and
the Los Angeles County Arts Commission partially support Red Hen Press.

Red Hen Press
www.redhen.org

Printed in Canada

First Edition

For

Obi
(Blair)
Ugochinyerem

Acknowledgements

David St. John, Blair Holt, Ron Gottesman, Carol Muske-Dukes, Steve Isioardi, Jeannette Lindsay, Kwame Dawes, Maurya Simon, Eloise Klein Healy, Amy Schroeder, PB Rippey, Richard Moore (who I unforgivably left out of GraceLand), Tanya Heflin, Joy Harjo, Kate Gale, Mark Cull and everyone at Red Hen.

My new family—Jacquie Wyatt, Bill Wyatt and Landon Holt.

Elliot Bay Book Company, Seattle for the unflagging support.

The Lannan Foundation, whose generosity helped make this book possible; thank you.

"Strange Fruit" and "Revelation" appear in *CALLALOO*.

"Constellations (III)" appears in *POOL*.

"Mary, Patterns" and "Dark Waters (III)" appear in *Poetry NZ*.

"Mary Magdalene As Marlene Dietrich" appears in *Velocity: An Apples & Snakes Anthology* (UK).

"Geography Lesson" appears in *Eclipse*.

"Dog Woman" appears in *The Seattle Review*.

"DeCasa's Aria – A Funk In D Minor," "Memoriam I," "Memoriam II," "Note to Self I," "The Annunciation," "Alchemy of Fire," "Towards Haunting," "Sunlight," and "Elegy" appear in *Mosaic*.

TABLE OF CONTENTS

Author's Note   11

Epiphany's Prologue
    The Ghosts of Us   15

Water Woman
    Dark Waters   19
    Dark Waters (II)   20
    River   21
    Labyrinths   22
    Constellations   23
    Fertile   24
    Dark Waters (III)   25
    Patterns   26
    Patterns (II)   27
    Constellations (II)   28
    Ritual   29
    Patterns (III)   30
    Chant   31

Fire Woman
    Wood   35
    La Brea Woman   36
    Gentle Fire   37
    Blue   38
    In the Middle of Dinner   40
    Toil   41
    Amina   42
    The Whipping   43
    Geography Lesson   44

Stone Woman
    De Casas' Aria – A Funk in D Minor   48
    The Book of Generations   50
    Memoriam I   53
    Memoriam II   54
    Note to Self (I)   56
    The Annunciation   57
    The Dream of the Rood   59

Alchemy of Fire   61
Towards Haunting   62
Note to Self (II)   63
The Golden Bough   65
Sunlight   66
Elegy   67
In the House of Spirits   68

Unholy Woman
Urinal Virgin   71
Mary Magdalene as Marlene Dietrich   72
Mrs. Lot   73
Dog Woman   74
Mary   78
Mary & Martha   79
Unholy Women   80
Lush   82
Flesh   87

Tree Woman
Prelude   91
Revelation   92
Poison Oak   93
Postcard   94
Ropes of Sand   95
Killing Zoë   96
Ada Mae   97
Body and Soul   98
Rag Doll   99
Strange Fruit   100

Epiphany's Epilogue
The Poet's Dream of Autonomy   103
Never More Than That   104

Notes   107

Author's Note

Portuguese

This book was born when I came across a remarkable sequence of paintings by ~~Spanish~~ artist Paula Rego. The sequence was called Dog Women, detailing women is several canine poses. At the time I was reading Rilke's *Dueno Elegies* and thinking about his construction of angels and what emblematic functions they served, and whose. This naturally led me to Baudelaire and his theories on dolls and their souls, and in a circuitous way, to the African lyric tradition and an examination of the way language, particularly among the Igbo, served function beyond communication: that it was in fact a moment, an event even, of philosophical excavation, a thrust towards the ineffable. This led me to ideas around sign and taboo, through De Casas' *The Devastation of the Indies*, La Malinche and finally to the ghosts that inform this book.

And what are these poems? Perhaps a vision quest into one soul, if one can use such words in polite company. An exploration of the patriarchal attempts to contain women and the failure of that containment? An attempt to come to the truth of women, an attempt that must fail. One poet's journey into the dark haunting of his own masculinity? I have only questions, no answers. In the end, these poems are their own reason for being, their own answer.

They are what they are, these poems.

Chris Abani
Los Angeles, 2004.

Epiphany's Prologue

Who bellows with this moan
Of a great melancholy ox?

Mother: The moon, it is the moon
In the Courtyard of the Dead

—Federico García Lorca

Death that cannot form until the shocked
tongue has given it permission.

—Djuana Barnes
Nightwood

THE GHOSTS OF US

I

This living with ghosts is our desire
to return. Their magnificence, like the moon
reflected, requires nothing beyond
their existence. Fetal fern unfurling dew-damp.
It is not so hard to love a ghost, David said.
Death is the thing you cannot fold into words.
It comes like water still as a garden pool and dark.
I am borne up light as an autumn leaf, floating.

epiphany

I have seen
blood, in clumps, blooming in rain
and I have forgotten how

to fly

II

There is such a thing as too much. The way
dead women fill a landscape.
But this is what their bodies are. An opportunity.
The tender way their blood charts it all.
And the haunting; nothing more.

a beautiful woman, eyes soft

the mystery, held in a sunflower
seed
fire of all life
promises not kept return to this place

I dream of ashes

Water Woman

The woman is doubly in shadow

—Gayatri Chakravorty Spivak
"Can the Subaltern Speak?"

All the dark women of history have lost their tongues.

—Yxta Maya Murray
The Conquest

DARK WATERS:

Jabu rabu jabu rabu jabu rabu

       Onu tom onu rom

Jabu rabu jabu rabu jabu rabu

       Onu tom onu rom

   Jabu rabu onu tom onu rom

Jabu rabu onu rom onu tom

     Jabu rabu hee! Jabu rabu hoo!

Jabu rabu onu tom onu rom

DARK WATERS (II):

Thrown to the other side of the river
      like sheltering from rain in a pond.

Falling—

    The terrible noise is silence.

And the earth never gets fat.

      Even the deepest eye cannot see the moon

But splutter, splutter is not fire.

     To those who would tie water down
ask: the water in the pot or the ocean?

RIVER:

The drumbeat changes.

                              The dance changes.

            A hunter eating mushrooms.

How to repay the gravedigger?

                  Tie up the corpse in grass cloth.

                  He went far away.
                  He went long ago.
                  He went before anybody came.
                  Which is the oldest?

The mouth knows no fear

                        But if hair is so easy to grow
                              why do turtles struggle so?

LABYRINTHS:

Let me cut the difficult knot.

      The King may be a lake

            but the breast is an intricate web

CONSTELLATIONS (II):

Take the secret road

Enter the cave

Reach for the ashes   The soft one reaches for the ashes

She does   Reaches

Throws a handful into the sky   A fistful

The fist is small   The fingers long

Grey, white, black

This is the secret road

How many?

Count your tongue with your teeth

FERTILE:

A stinging whip.

Beads of silver.

War shines in his eye.

Fire in his eye fire in his mouth fire on the roof.

Strong without flesh. Bone. Blood.

Ripping without hands.

A soft kiss.

DARK WATERS (III):

Born from a flower

     Its face darkens the world

   To be forgotten

       The gazelle's leap before the snare

Who broke the string for me?

PATTERNS:

The heart is the dance

      If you steal a drum where will you play it?

The moving arm stems from the body

   A hot thing

Over there smoke goes up
         Over there smoke goes up

      Can you catch hold of a shadow?
      Can you follow the road until it ends?

An ugly person cannot be put back in the womb

      An ancient name cannot be cooked and eaten

And the dying of the heart is unshared

   A hot thing

PATTERNS (II):

Family names, like flowers
                bloom in clusters.

The human heart is a sea
            but what does a river weigh?

The sweat of a dog ends in its hair.

            Is god with a watery nose really an ox?

How little things defeat us.

CONSTELLATIONS (III):

Riddle me this—

Water standing up   Water in the seamless gourd   Water in the elephant's leg.

Flame on the hill

Seh!

Little things that defeat us

The house in which one cannot turn around

A lake, on the body, surrounded by reeds

Two rows of white horses on a red hill

The roof always drips rain

And this thing is like dew showering down around

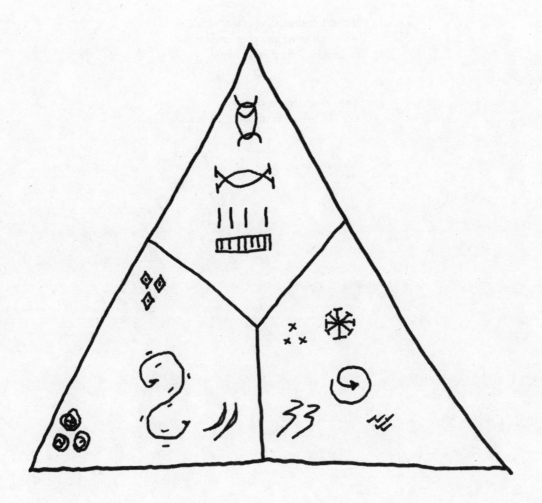

PATTERNS (III):

Certain knowledge came first—

Water, like the spring of the womb,
    all brine and then iron
rusting into the flow of blood.

Then mud, its personality as
    obvious as the silence of rocks.

CHANT:

It was the hornbill that spoke it.
In the nothing, becoming nothing,
begetting nothing; this is everything.

The world is old, the world is new

How does the darkness hide?
In the nothing, becoming nothing,
begetting nothing; this is everything.

The world is old, the world is new

The sun is no bigger than a crab.
In the nothing, becoming nothing,
begetting nothing; this is everything.

The world is old, the world is new

Hot soup is devoured from the edges.
In the nothing, becoming nothing,
begetting nothing; this is everything.

The world is old, the world is new

The blood sign is red; burning like fire.
In the nothing, becoming nothing,
begetting nothing; this is everything.

The world is old, the world is new

It has no name; silence is its name.
In the nothing, becoming nothing,
begetting nothing; this is everything.

The world is old, the world is new.

Fire Woman

You may forget but

Let me tell you
This: someone in
Some future time
Will think of us.

—Sappho

WOOD

Chips fly tangential to the swing of the axe.
Grandmother's smile reveals it is good.
Uneven runnels mark the emerging figure
with the things of life that temper us.

Carved with the sacredness reserved
for the spoken, glottal, it is caught
in the back of her throat, warmed
by the heat of her heart

like hot palm-oil smeared thick
on split skin: healing.
But some things work better in song.

Like the bridge leading to the next verse.
Still, poets lash words across chasms,
sway, delicate as a butterfly wing
beating past the oppression of a dewdrop.

LA BREA WOMAN

(Page Museum, L.A.)

To approximate

This is the measure of balance
Perspective, the line of sight
The hair is a full growth; compelling
This is how the eye is trained
The heart becoming a collaborator

Note:

Discovered in pit 10.
9,000 years old.
Wisdom tooth in jaw.
Upper leg bone indicates
Height
4 feet 8 inches.
About eighteen.

Note:

Hers, the only human remains.
She was most probably murdered
ceremoniously buried in the tar pits.

This is the angle of sight
The way the eye is trained
This is the full measure

To approximate the dimensions of a body

GENTLE FIRE

My sister does not envy me the fame
accorded the performance of my pain.
She who since fifteen has been betrayed
by a body bent on devouring itself.

Instead she loves the child they said
she would never have. But her eyes
tell me she knows—What a luxury
to choose your own suffering.

BLUE

I

Africans in the hold fold themselves
to make room for hope. In the afternoon's
ferocity, tar, grouting the planks like the glue
of family, melts to the run of a child's licorice stick.

Wet decks crack, testing the wood's mettle.
Distilled from evaporating brine, salt
dusts the floor, trickling with the measure
into time and the thirst trapped below.

II

The captain's new cargo of Igbos disturbs him.
They stand, computing the swim back to land.
Haitians still say: *Ibo pend'c or' a ya!*
But we do not hang ourselves in cowardice.

III

Sold six times on the journey to the coast,
once for a gun, then cloth, then iron
manilas, her pride was masticated like husks
of chewing sticks, spat from morning-rank mouths.

Breaking loose, edge of handcuffs held high
like the blade of a vengeful axe, she runs
across the salt scratch of deck,
pain deeper than the blue inside a flame.

IV

The sound, like the break of bone
could have been the Captain's skull
or the musket shot dropping her
over the side, her chains wrapped
around his neck in dance.

IN THE MIDDLE OF DINNER

my mother put down her knife and fork,
pulled her wedding ring from its groove,
placing it contemplatively on her middle
finger. So natural was the move,
so tender, I almost didn't notice.
Five years, she said, five years, once a week,
I wrote a letter to your father. And waited
until time was like ash on my tongue.
Not one letter back, not a single note.
She sighed, smiling, the weight gone. This
prime rib is really tender, isn't it? she asked.

TOIL

She squatted over banana leaves slaked
by the fall of her broken water. The farm
deserted as she severed the umbilical.
Swaddled; the child in the inside out clean
of her lappa, the after-birth carefully wrapped
in the banana leaves of birth. The child
had come early, before her hoe broke earth, so
she gathered wood into a bundle. Its heft
on her head would balance the child
on her back. Why waste the day?

AMINA

It is there in the controlled rage of her sword,
The powerful grip of her thighs directing her mount,
Her throne spreading buttocks,
In her six foot plus frame vibrant like a stallion's kick.
Zaria's queen. Amina, like Bodecia's Celtic rampant defiance,
Did what no man was woman enough to—
Even as a child she was her father's favorite son.

THE WHIPPING

Only one other thing had cored her like this.
His gentle tongue lashing the swell of her pudenda,
frantic as a swimmer drowning at sea
until the sound forced from her was silence.

GEOGRAPHY LESSON

To the Igbo everyone is family, everything
is connected, Grandmother explained.
Like the weave of this raffia mat, we intertwine,
see? This is the world to the Igbo.

Nodding, the German anthropologist licked
her pencil in concentration and wrote:

To the Igbo, the world is flat like a mat.

Stone Woman

Such is the power of the image:
It heals only those who know what it is.
For everyone else, it is an illness.

—Roberto Calasso

Were I to recount the vile acts committed here,
the exterminations, the massacres, the cruelties,
the violence and sinfulness against God and the King of Spain,
I would write a very big book, but this will have to wait
for another time, God willing.

—Bartolome De Casas
The Devastation of the Indies: A Brief Account

THE WAY OF THE CROSS

The way of the Cross is a devotion to the Sacred Passion, in which we accompany, in spirit, our Blessed Lord in His sorrowful journey from the house of Pilate to Calvary, and recall to mind, with sorrow and love, all that took place from the time when he was condemned to death to His being laid in the tomb. There are fourteen Stations, or places, in the Way of the Cross, at which something took place. At each Station we should say the Our Father and the Hail Mary with love and sorrow for our sins, meditating on the suffering of our Lord represented to us at the Station.

Indulgences

Those who may devoutly make the Stations of the Cross, may gain a plenary indulgence.

Those who are lawfully hindered from making the Stations of the Cross, may gain the same indulgence if they read and meditate on the Passion and Death of our Lord for at least one half-hour.

Indulgences in accord with the new "Euchiridion Inulgentiarum"
From *The Way of the Cross* by Saint Alphonsus Liguori. Catholic Book Publishing Co., N.Y.

Jesus is Condemned to Death

V: We adore you, O Christ, and we bless you
R: Because by Your holy Cross, You have redeemed the world.

Consider how Jesus was unjustly condemned by Pilate to die on the Cross.

My Jesus it was not Pilate, no, it was my sins that condemned You to die.

De Casas' Aria – A Funk in D Minor

I

We had to invent a hate for it.
There is no way to decapitate a child tenderly
No etiquette on how to feed a man
To dogs hungry with their master's denial.

We made of it a place to live, a castle,
But there is a black flower that grows
In a field of green, and for all its emerald blaze
All you see is the coal of that flower.

Though we pretend they are not human
Our damnation is the plague that we have become
Hearts blacker than that field of flowers
And we have only this.

II

And though you confront the mystery
Between altar lights and the weight of beads
And though you mea culpa all night
The thing that it is

Will not be wished away
Nor the vertigo.
And it is not what it reveals to you
It is the thing hid

And this is the wisdom of simple things
Like a spoon, a bowl, a hoe
And the heavy fall of fruit.

❋

At the Cross her station keeping,
Stood the mournful mother weeping,
Close to Jesus to the last.

STATION II

Jesus Carries His Cross

V: We adore you, O Christ, and we bless you
R: Because by Your holy Cross, You have redeemed the world.

Consider how Jesus, in making this journey with the cross on His shoulders, thought of us.

My Beloved Jesus, I embrace all the tribulations You have destined for me until death.

The Book of Generations

I

Cimatl and Tenepal begat
Malinali
Cimatl passed on to the great darkness
and Tenepal remarried and bore a son.
Malinali
herb, white feathered fan, yarn of a riber
stood next in the throne's shadow.
Tenepal, with a mother's love
sought her son, not her daughter
to ascend the throne.
Malinali,
headstrong and proud
was not her mother's daughter
but her father's heart

Malinali
was a woman.

II

Birthright stolen
Malinali
was sold to merchants.
Indentured, she traveled everywhere

with these pochtecas.
In Tabasco, they sold her to the chief of Chocan.
She learned Mayan with the ease
of survival and her exceptional skills
earned her property and the suffix, tzing.

Malinali became Malintzin

III

There were always men
in her life. This time, Cortez.
And she, the most gifted in the Mayan
King's seraglio, was the gift,
along with nineteen others.
Baptized the next dawn by Friar De Olemedo,

Malinali-Malintzin became Marina.

IV

Skills, linguistic too,
brought her to Cortez's attention.
She became his interpreter.

Was this the choice?
Did she become the pot mixer?
Liberator of those under the crushing
hand of the Aztecs?
Or traitor to her people, selling her soul
and the souls of those who had sold her?

V

And for Marina, what gift?
The name La Malinche. A volcano. An old house
decaying by the sea. The scorn of her people.
A son, Don Martin Cortez,
prime meztizo, the first begotten son.
And death as a woman.

❈

Through her heart, His sorrow sharing
All His bitter anguish bearing,
Lo! the piercing sword had passed!

STATION III

Jesus Falls the First Time

Consider this first fall of Jesus under His Cross.

My Beloved Jesus, it is not the weight of the Cross, but my sins which made you suffer so much pain.

Memoriam I

The picture of La Malinche
on an imagined movie poster
wears the face of Salma Hayek,
and all the lust of Sophia Loren.

This movie poster Marina is all
we dare. Gorgons are too frightening
to contemplate; mutilated by our fear.

In truth, she was a child.
Fifteen when given to Cortez
from a people who bought her
when she was barely five.

But this is what men are like.

This is my knife

Here, the cloth my mother wove

From yarn I spun

This? This is a needle of bone,
threading like marrow

This is bread, soft as my body.
Here. Take it. A memory.

This? A jar of oil, seasoned
By my hand
Here. Dip your bread. A memory.

This? This is the stone
Where I ground myself away.

Touch it. Touch me.
Knife. Cloth. Needle. Bread. Oil. Stone.

I will not die.

This is the memory of me.

✳

O, how sad, and sore distressed,
Now she, that Mother Blessed
Of the sole-begotten One.

53

STATION IV

Jesus Meets His Sorrowful Mother

V: We adore You, O Christ, and we bless You.
R: Because by Your holy Cross, You have redeemed the world.

Consider the meeting of the Son and the Mother, which took place on this journey.

My most loving Jesus grant me the grace of a truly devoted love for Your most holy Mother.

Memoriam II

I

I am this stone in the middle of the road.
Blessed by the fall of her sweat,
by the fall of her sorrow,
as she walks this life's path.

I am a shadow in the window
            waiting

II

I am this seed kicked by her feet
I am this seed; I am this star.
Where does night stop being light?
Where does love cease to be anything but this?

I am the dust settling
            on the artifacts of your life
            Barely leaving a trace

III

Did he ever touch her face in public?
Or was that particular tenderness a place
he never traveled to? This much
I can tell: *It is hard to remain human.*

            The slight depression
            in the chair
watching you sleep at night

IV

I suppose you could say that.
But candles will burn with the pleasure
of their own crackling.
And if the incense censer is God's pipe,
how lazy of him not to get his own vices.

I am a ghost
            made by your shame
wishing my dead were here
            to save me

V

I cradled your words
to my breast
Lie by lie
But all children must
be weaned

Her silence watches me; stoic
as a mud granary guarding a night field.
And no one else I've known died of love.
Still this is her inheritance: This patch of sky
shredded by swallow's wings; and my art.

※

Woe-begone, with heart's prostration
Mother meek, the bitter Passion
Saw she of her glorious Son.

Simon Helps Jesus to Carry the Cross

V: We adore you, O Christ, and we bless you
R: Because by Your holy Cross, You have redeemed the world.

Consider Simon the Cyrenian, constrained to carry the Cross behind our Lord.

My dear Jesus, I will not refuse the Cross as the Cyrenian did.

Note to Self (I)

It tastes like something.
                              All of it.

Remember Susan said to you after your reading –

    I thought these poems were about women.

No, you said. They are about ghosts.
        The evacuation of women.
                        No, you said, they are about men.

No, you said.

                        This is what they are.

These Poems.

                            ❋

    Who could mark, from tears refraining,
    Christ's dear Mother uncomplaining
    In so great a sorrow bowed?

STATION VI

Veronica Wipes the Face of Jesus

V: We adore you, O Christ, and we bless you
R: Because by Your holy Cross, You have redeemed the world.

Consider how the holy woman Veronica presented Him with a towel, with which He wiped His adorable face.

My beloved Jesus, Your face was beautiful before, but in this journey it has lost all its beauty.

The Annunciation

Candles gutter under the intensity of her gaze
dispelling a votive passion; fire,
into dripping wax; yet hot.

Perdóname mi amor, estoy débil.

This was not the annunciation she had planned.
No fallen angel to lead her by the hand
between nodded sleep and counted breath,

each precious, holding the measure
of her prayer, the unspoken. Desire,
the hush between bell-tolls, falls softer than morning.

Once chasing butterflies into a field
she came upon subjects who bowed. That moment,
she wished insignificance was all she had.

Perdóname mi amor, estoy débil.

Night settles in blue, warming itself
to the full bodied black of good coffee
on the unsteady flames of the votive candles.

She gathers her rosary with the echo of pebbles
collected on the edge of pagan Sundays by a meditative
sea; their smoothness the real thing.

The assurance: life will become more life. Unbroken
circles or curves hold it with heart-breaking tenderness,
yet with the power to defy time; eternal.

Perdóname mi amor, estoy débil.

But there are things that can only be
approximated, like the curve of a bowl,
the dance of tomorrow, new life, new hope.

She would hold him, withholding from him
even as his wave overwhelmed her rock.
Struggling to be brave, this time, she would whisper.

Perdóname mi amor, estoy débil.

❋

Who, unmoved, behold her languish,
Underneath His cross of anguish,
'Mid the fierce, unpitying crowd?

Jesus Falls the Second Time

V: We adore You, O Christ, and we bless You.
R: Because by Your holy Cross, You have redeemed the world.

Consider the second fall of Jesus under the Cross.

My most gentle Jesus, how many times You have pardoned me!

The Dream of the Rood

I

La Llorona; in the darkness of arteries, she lurks
with the patience of a fermenting hate.
Denial is key to eradication, so her face first
is obliterated, the empty hug of her cowl's shadow
and all we see is the sum of our terror—
Nails, long and silvery in the imagined moonlight.

I am the wood of your lives, your windhold,
your lintel, your chair, your board, your death,
your life, your bed. The post of a mid-day's
    yawning lean.
I am the wood of your lives. The hearth,
    the fire,
the smoke, the warmth, the cross, the sacrifice.

II

A river of sighs pours from the cut,
everything belonging to the heart. Desire
mixing with blood in this season of milk.
The world is filled with the death of a single woman.
And nothing encompasses the moment.
Not a homeless woman shuffling behind a cart,
nor words like truth, beauty or even genocide.
The moon on wet tarmac is a lie.

I am the wood of your lives, crossroad in
    complex grain.
I hold the sacrifice of your days, the dreams of
    your nights,
the blood of your fear, the greed
    of your offering,
your garden's lost delight,

III

This is the measure of my faith—
A coyote circling my car three times,
Joshua trees falling back from the road,
this land reclaiming me in rock and
I bite down on this lie and swallow.
If this death proves anything—there is power
even in the words of an ordinary woman.

Pillar of day, post of night, the
    wood of your lives.
Ah, smoke me to nothingness.

✳

For His people's sins rejected,
She her Jesus, unprotected,
Saw with thorns, with scourges rent.

STATION VIII

The Women of Jerusalem Weep Over Jesus

V: We adore You, O Christ, and we bless You
R: Because by Your holy Cross, You have redeemed the world.

Consider how those women wept with compassion at seeing Jesus in such a pitiable state.

My Jesus, laden with sorrows, I weep for the offenses I have committed against You.

Alchemy of Fire

Seeing the fascination of fire
in the child's eye, she floated the candle's stub
across the fountain's wave. It rode
on the upside down picture
of the Virgin of the Sacred Heart,
accompanied by the ripples of her song.
The storm brewing the crossing unleashed
in a whip's lick across her back;
and then the hanging.

Suspended, she saw only the fascination
of death in the child's eye.
Fighting the rope's bite, she sung
it to the refuge of a heartbeat's shadow.

※

Saw her Son from judgment taken,
Her belov'd in death forsaken
Till His Spirit forth He sent.

STATION IX

Jesus Falls the Third Time

V: We adore You, O Christ, and we bless You.
R: Because by Your holy Cross, You have redeemed the world.

Consider the third fall of Jesus Christ.

My outraged Jesus, give me strength sufficient to conquer all human respect.

Towards Haunting

There is the contradiction of forests.
Sorrow tender with the regret of rain—
and salt is the taste of the fall.

Though you have the wand
we hold the world
Our womb

What if I carve my name into temple steps,
draw my faith in stone, on every wall?
Things without a name are terrifying.

Though you point
We are the destination

Yet grass can hold the rain in fluted stems.
If the soul exists, why does it not haunt
evil's sleep, the nightmare of its killer?

Though you rage like storms
We are the power

How it dissipates in the faith of light.
Waves on the beach wash meditatively.
Lengthening with evening's stretch,

Though you still grow
we wear the face of God

licking the last of light
from the walls, return the ghosts.

❀

Fount of love and holy sorrow
Mother, may my spirit borrow
Somewhat of your woe profound

STATION X

Jesus Is Stripped of His Garments

V: We adore You, O Christ, and we bless You
R: Because by Your holy Cross, You have redeemed the world.

Consider the violence with which the executioners stripped Jesus.

My innocent Jesus, help me strip myself of all affection to things of earth.

Note to Self (II)

[These are the facts]

> I should know, I have read
> all the books on the subject.

And if she lived in a small English village?
With a name like La Malinche?
Not hardly.

> A woman with her reputation?
> Frankly I don't know
> what to think.

What is the measure of a heart torn?
We pause and listen to time passing.

> Gather all the desiccated hearts.
> Smoke them in a fire
> until they become nothing –
> Only hot breath on night's face.

Ah, let them grieve, let them.

> What can you say about a life you cannot
> remember?
> Yet remember this life you cannot speak,
> or speak as a lie.

But this much is true:
I have only lied to those I love.

❋

Unto Christ, with pure emotion,
Raise my contrite heart's devotion,
Love to read in every wound.

STATION XI

Jesus is Nailed to the Cross

V: We adore You, O Christ, and we bless You
R: Because by Your holy Cross, You have redeemed the world.

Consider how Jesus offered to His Eternal Father the sacrifice of His death for our salvation.

My Jesus! loaded with contempt, nail my heart to Your feet.

The Golden Bough

We are born like this:
melancholy; the call of a lost gull
tearing night with the burn of it,

cracking our wings to the dust
of old parchments stored in caves,
falling, grain by grain.

And death can come like this.
In slow increments.
But sometimes, we feel

it necessary to preface
it with a thunderstorm, rain washing
in an imagined purity.

And this is the nub:

we oft think vision the bigger.
Everything a landscape can see.
But sound fills spaces not yet dreamed.

※

Those five wounds on Jesus smitten,
Mother! in my heart be written,
Deep as in your own they be.

STATION XII

Jesus is Raised Upon the Cross, and Dies

V: We adore You, O Christ, and we bless You
R: Because by Your holy Cross, You have redeemed the world.

Consider how Jesus, after three hours' Agony on the Cross, bows His head, and dies.

O my dying Jesus, I kiss devoutly the Cross on which You died for love of me.

Sunlight

The old woman dies on the sunny porch.
Feeble hands, palms up in lap, collect what
light she can, for the darkness to cross.

❋

You, my Savior's Cross who bear,
And your Son's rebuke who share,
Let me share them both with you!

66

STATION XIII

Jesus is Taken Down from the Cross

V: We adore You, O Christ, and we bless You
R: Because by Your holy Cross, You have redeemed the world.

Consider how Joseph and Nicodemus, took Him down from the Cross,
and placed Him in the arms of His afflicted Mother.

O mother of sorrow, for the love of this Son, accept me for your servant, and pray to Him for me.

Elegy

A country churchyard, but no elegy
for the dead. My feet scuff their faces.
Ten thousand Chumash feed this soil, souls
marked only by the flowers they push up.

And the rest is death, and only death.

The one who lived with birds, Juana Maria,
her true name lost to all but dolphins
sighs to the wind from the black plaque
with an embossed compass, riveted to stone.

And the rest is death, and only death.

If I could match the rage of prophets
I would call down fire; righteous, righteous fire.
In the softness of skin, I turn to my lover.
If only I could wear her heart next to mine.
And love is a cannibalistic feast.

But the rest is death, and death alone.

My blood is the cry of water
unable to slake its own thirst.

Imagine a love this complete —
Dare.
Imagine it, compressed between:
Fear?

But mine is not a quiet grave.
It sits on the hillside of the heart

collecting something that is not dust,
halo darker than a monk's cowl.

And there are no names
for the things we carry to the grave.

The oarsman must be paid.
Your heart, poeta, the levy.

✻

In the Passion of my Maker,
Be my sinful soul partaker,
Weep till death, and keep with you

STATION XIV

Jesus is Laid in the Sepulcher

V: We adore You, O Christ, and we bless You
R: Because by Your holy Cross, You have redeemed the world.

Consider how the disciples carried the body of Jesus to bury it, accompanied by His holy Mother.

Oh, my buried Jesus, I kiss the stone that encloses you.

In The House of Spirits

I

A house alone by the sea
A house on a bluff overlooking the sea
All around, the ghostly call of waves to unrelenting
stone, like time beating itself to death
on the indifference of the universe

A Love Frustrated

II

This house lonely by the sea
This house on a bluff overlooking the sea
has no roof, and though weathered walls sun
in this brightness, the damp fills it all—
This house, this bluff, this day, this sea

Un amor frustrado.

⁂

Mine with you be that sad station,
There to watch the great Salvation
Wrought upon th' atoning Tree.

Unholy Woman

Imagine a thin woman
Before bread was invented,
Playing a harp of wheat in the fields.

—Carol Muske-Dukes

What motivates us is mystery,
How the aloof stone desires more than anything
To be opened, shivering and wet with love.

—Joy Harjo

URINAL VIRGIN

In my friend's bathroom the mystery—Why
a urinal? And why Our Lady of Guadalupe
leaning back in the niche surrounded by rust
that won't wash away? A dried flower and a candle
burn with an uncertain flame. Instinctively,
without thinking, much like San Juan Diego I pull
myself from my boxers, my penis nodding
to the serpent she tramples underfoot; familial. And
she smiles. The one who spoke to Juan in Nahuatl
calling herself Coatlaxopeuh, she who crushes serpents.

MARY MAGDALENE AS MARLENE DIETRICH

I

If God had any dress sense, he would look like this:
The blonde hair swept high and to the left.
The full red pout, the wrist teasing the world
with the Gitane smoldering like the slow fires of hell.
And black. The suit. Or the bustier. And the hat.
And the voice calling like Ka from The Jungle Book:
"Trust in me, just in me, close your eyes, trust in me."

II

Haunting smoke-faded-velvet-curtained-cabaret-stages,
voice thick with the sediment of regret and squandered vice.
Hooded lids, pursed lips and the cigarette, always the cigarette.
Could you bear to look into these eyes?
This body, once filled with the thick pulse of God's love
veils a universe collapsed in on itself like an endless night,
or the simple shadow cast on a tender shoulder by an earring.

MRS. LOT

Were it not for the curves in the pillar
I wouldn't have known her.
Are you? Really? Tell me.
Voice all tears and salt, she said:
I remember nothing.

DOG WOMAN

It's like flying in your dreams, she said. You empty
Yourself out and just lift off. Soar. It's like that.

⁂

Red.   Red.   Red.

    Just that word. Sometimes.

⁂

Yang & Yin. Like twins tumbling through summer.
     He, the rooster crowing sun; desperate—afraid—
       As only men can be.

And Yin? Let's say she has long hair—
     No, that won't work. If we are to believe
the ancient Chinese, she was a dog
        howling moon.

⁂

When I counted out the pills, it was a slowing down.
     Like the delay between when the car goes through
the dip and your stomach falls away—
      And won't stop.

⁂

Of course it was because she didn't fit my mold.
So I punished her. And why? And why? And why?
     You did it, I said. You did it.
Wouldn't fill my world.

⁂

And eventually we all kill our mothers.
Their eyes a tenderness that doesn't flinch
     from it. Knowing. Eventually.

＊

What else is there?

＊

Paula's paintings are real. The women thick, visceral, rude,
like stubborn cliffs the sea cannot contain—or drown.

＊

Or dogs. And such as these drove Homer to despair—
And his cry: Oh to see! To see! To see!

＊

So Paula says: To be a dog woman is bestial is good.
        Eating, snarling.
Utterly believable.
                Gross.

＊

Like when Cesaria Evora breaks your heart with a smile
        all melancholy and sea and salt.

            Assim 'm ta pidi mar
            Pa 'l leva 'me pa 'me ca voeta

And it doesn't matter that you don't know what
        the words mean. Some things are beyond that.

＊

So. Tanya bought the record because Cesaria's face
        is beautiful with all the lost love of the world
and darker than the blue of the sun setting over the Atlantic.

It's in the angle of light washing her hair
with sun into a puddle that catches in the throat

The wood deck creaks from the weight
of all that air and sun and silence
Water chuckling in the tiny fountain in the corner
holding up the song of wind chimes and flies

And it's all here. Fire. Water. Stone. Wood.

※

All caught up in Yeats and the cuckoo
        that wasn't a real bird but cried
with all the agony of the desire for flight
hemmed by wooden wings, and springs and cogs.

I think.

※

Or looking for Rilke—
        How the panther is like the rage
of a doll's soul caught in the body: but
to say: under an open window, a violin

Accomplishment though is another matter—
Just ask Baudelaire and so I
        thought I could do it.

Necromancer, necromancer, necromancer
        make me a mate
only one of my ribs pray take.

So why won't women fit into that space?

※

Is that why in the photograph David plays
an inflatable lyre? Does his smile make it all artifice?

※

But life is this and it will not
be contained. The Igbo say:
No one can outrun their shadow.
And this is good. This is hope.
Because, or maybe, we cannot outrun love.

※

To drive down a road, she said. Until it stops
at the edge of the sea. An ocean vast and immense,
she said. If you are lucky, she said. It fills you.

MARY

I know this thing, unspeakable, is piety.
  The notion
that the divine's desire, lust even
   shapes itself into the swell—
The gesture, like a fruit torn from a limb
  torn swiftly.

A lie? Perhaps
  it was not God's vibrance
that filled her chamber with a light
  desperate to be born
but another; but other than Joseph.

We will never know if this thing
leaning into piety can be or not.
Unable to let out its breath,
  yet eased by the breath
of hot bread, a warm bed, milk boiling on a hearth.

MARY & MARTHA

Night would be perfect.
    A slow burning hearth
throwing sparks at the forbidden
pillow of leavened bread
      falls short of all that is desired.
As does oil—even the sweetened
or the perfumed emollient
rubbed into the feet of God
as he reposed by the flame,
      fanning the adoration of one sister

while the other, Martha, caught
in the net of hospitality
pokes at the lazy fire cooking outside
hurrying it to boil the lamb.
      The hope; seasoning potatoes—
Of course there was salt too, always salt.
The glowing tip' of the poker begs metaphor.
Cigarette? The burning point of God's love?
The rivet of sacrifice? A bitter ember?
      But this thing is older than that.
They are sisters
      and the savior is just another man
their brother have brought home.

UNHOLY WOMEN

But of course these poems are

about men,

which we become by defining how
we are not women
and
so becoming

a shadow devouring the light to find the limits

which is what Richard Pryor would have told Joan of Arc
in a joke funnier for being sexist

"It's a man thang."

And of course there is God

and its problematic relationship to light

not to mention the question
of permission

Who builds the box, the shape?

It makes sense that Jesus, the new man 2,000 years ago

was a carpenter.

You need that craft, the precision of measurement

angles of angels

who incidentally are never women.

Just ask the Romans, who called them Angelo, Angelus

never Angela—

that lie was coined by a dissident nun hiding
her feminism under the cover of rapture

but

is it enough to announce yourself?
To beat your chest in contrition calling

Mea culpa! Mea culpa?

Guilt can never be enough
Mere intent—where is its purpose?

Yet there are no answers

there are only lines that disappear

into horizons that girder us with safety

just as there is no way to end this poem.

LUSH

There is a poem in here somewhere.

❋

And the rain takes its pleasure from the mud.

❋

I was old enough to know better.

        Did that angry kick to my sister's stomach
start it all?

❋

And over, and over, her body devours her. Pain
        soaking her soul.
      Heavy, it hangs from her tired shoulders.

If I could, sweet one. If I could.
        But men have no language for it—
The suffering of others.

❋

There must be a way to face the storm.

        There must be a way to avoid the storm.

There must be a way to learn the storm.

        There must be a way.

There must be a face.

        There must be a storm.

❋

Necesito del mar porque me ensena.

    And I do
        Need the ocean to teach me.
I will not pretend here,
the line belongs to Pablo Neruda

    yet for all that

        living is hard for me.

❋

Do you remember Tadeusz, David?

    Those lines?

That old woman who
Is pulling a goat on a rope
Is more necessary
And more precious
Than the seven wonders of the world
Whoever thinks and feels
That she is not necessary
He is guilty of genocide.

❋

I meant to write you a letter

    I meant to tell you a lie.

❋

For all the women I have known

    for all the tenderness I am capable
the darkness in me is still a man.

※

Because I believed

       I remember you as you were

that night

※

It would be easy to give in

       to the contemplation of you

like the man in Picasso's painting.

   You are the sea

       There is only the swallowing of life for you.

※

February 14

Dearest,

Ideally it should be raining. And cool, though not cold. Dark. Night. Outside, flowers revel in the shower, washing petals clean and chattering like African women gathered by a stream to beat their husbands in the pound of cloth on rock; and to draw comfort from gossip shared like tidbits of sweet-meats. And.

※

This thing is not death.

     Only its pretence

※

They are leading the Zebu to the abattoir
horns spiking evening's mantle,
humps slumping sadly.

Their eyes betray the knowledge.
      Their resonant lows forgive us as they pass.
(They are cows, pull yourself together, man!)

          ✳

That smell?

      Kerosene on rain-wet earth.

          ✳

The smell of oysters

      and slippery too

sweet. So sweet.

          ✳

I have given it much thought—

      My pimp name.

Big Daddy C.

          ✳

Did I ever tell you about my Aunt Molly?

      Big, buxom, the usual clichés?

How she would go fishing with my uncle. Sit. Read in the cold. While he stared out

85

at the empty water. Waiting.

Tea. Sandwiches.

Passed silently.

Then she levering her bulk into the sidecar, nearly tipping him over
on the motorcycle. And at her feet, still slick from life, the eels
he had caught.

Oh how she hated fish.

How.

※

And did I tell you that she died most impolitely?
Right there on the toilet seat.
Heart couldn't take the strain, they said.

Did I mention that she was so big they had to get the fire-brigade to cut
the doorframe from the wall to get her out;

and the ambulance crew looked away

embarrassed by the thick pad clotting in the ball of her panties.

Such a disgrace, we laugh every time.

FLESH

Maria said:

> Don't you hate watermelon when it doesn't taste
> right? It is made worse because it looks so good,
> but when you bite into it, it's like the sugar left
> just before you got there.

Mother:

> Is love only the dying of water?

Tree Woman

I will not see it!

Tell the moon to come
For I do not want to see the blood
—Federico García Lorca

Torso slit neatly as an envelop,
The flesh folded back in awe
—Kimiko Hahn

PRELUDE

There is a story—I cannot tell it.

Remembering is not always good.

This is not my story—I shouldn't tell it—these cannot be my words.

Still:
A stranger is a better judge of fairness between twins.

This is everybody's story—we must tell it.

And.
Shame is finding ourselves in the details.

REVELATION

The memory:

       A dog licking the wail
       of a violin from evening's face
       doesn't ring true.

Yet:

they're finding bodies everyday now

           one clutching grass one

   the mud.

And:

       In this dusk, this gathering of shadows
       around slow burning oil lanterns,
       mosquitoes lulling day to sleep—

Lies can no longer be told.

POISON OAK

In the blue shadows we call night. Yes.
We *call* night. Why else do we pretend dark?
A line falling in thick black down the page
is the middle—like the lynching rope
holding our shame in suspense between

all that is good; all that is fecund.

There is something true in this moment,
not beautiful, never transcendental,
fed to flames and anger. Anatomically
as empty as an effigy,
the corpse's defiance denies the lie:

Love is apart from all things.

POSTCARD

Dear Janice,

This is the nigger maid who tried to steal Bill.
The lump dangling is the unborn thing they conceived.
If you look at the mob Bill is in the foreground,
marked for you to see. All else is fine and little
Jessica is doing well. Write soon.

Mary Louisa

ROPES OF SAND

The tree where she danced with the wind
neck leashed by a choker of hemp;
its fruits, surprisingly not bitter
but deeply sweet and refreshing
with the taste of history,
is framed in my window at dusk.

KILLING ZOË

(or seven questions)

Do women come to death differently?

Should the death of a woman mean more?
Life equals life, no?

But to submit?
To your love?
Killing you?

ADA MAE

The seed from this tree will wing
in some bird's beak. Fall. Grow on soil

alien as a soul trapped behind glass.
Will it tell the story of you?

Or will it forget you as fast as water
straining through a colander.

And in the whisper of the wind in the leaves
I can't help but feel cold in this silence.

Perhaps this madness is mine alone.
A dog howling to the moon.

BODY AND SOUL

Materials?

Trees; or at least wood.
      Rope, also bindings.
Blades; the cruelty of steel.
      Stones? These still remain optional,
but trustworthy.

(But if polemics, even emotion,
      be evacuated
how do we respect the eruptions of memory,
      the integrity of the fragment
even as we move through the sweep? The arc.
      No. The flow?)

History.

RAG DOLL

For a bet I imagine.

    A dare seems insufficient prompt—

How much the wager?

                  Dime? Nickel? Penny?

Maybe.

    Shrieks bouncing off hot sidewalks

they run up and twirl the foot

of the body

              swinging from the street—

light, misting in a halo

    and her shadow is a fool

flirting with the concrete.

STRANGE FRUIT

1

Her skeleton was a pendulum.
A forgotten wind chime.
She hung, full of something
that wasn't quite promise—

2

The blood dried quickly in the sand,
but sadness, like the buzzing of bees,
troubled the afternoon for days.

3

A fly landed with the weight of sorrow
on the dying woman's nose; her rasping
breath grooming its wings—

4

The dog's affectionate lick of her dangling
foot was spiced by the blood on her toe.

5

But shadows are gossiping in the sand
among the trees. And death,
darkening features like the hard
of old wood, is here.

Epiphany's Epilogue

You say I am repeating
Something I have said before.
I shall say it again.
Shall I say it again?

—T.S. Eliot

Yet the effect at last was of a woman
Constructed entirely of evening shadows.

—David St. John

The Poet's Dream of Autonomy

Even Baudelaire knew the folly
imbuing dolls with a soul
beyond our making, even
with his "Some reflections on Dolls."

Rilke's angels wear a terrifying
beauty betraying faith:
the knowledge of the true face of God.

Still I winnow, whittle really; everything
in flakes, or tender coils of wood, falls away
until no part remains that is surely you.

And what there is, no more tangible
than an echo riding canyon walls
whispers: beloved, beloved epiphany.

epiphany

when asked, grandmother said

she saw no sun; only its eye

· There are time-honored ways to die

all gods eat souls

their greed an angry sea

The darkness, a sea of stars

II

Never More Than That

Did you think you had a say?
That somehow the thing you set out
to create, turned counterpoint, by a will
beyond even your largest imagining,
monstrous, devouring you,
could be any more than this?

Did you think I had not your language?
Your skill at words? Felt perhaps necessary
to the process. Necessary to what must be?

Listen, if you wait long enough by the river
your enemies will come floating by: all.
Reign in your heart, humble yourself
before the knowledge that my existence,
as Epiphany, as every woman,
is as inevitable as life; as death—

it moves, we dance
one step behind,
like the echo of a drumbeat.

                          gather in myths
                              like dry clothes from a line
holding up a rainy afternoon

heaven is harder than a cloud

Alas! Alas!

Doves bring no respite

the legends tell we could fly

salt is the scatter of the fall—sankofa

                            if we dance, if we dance

my dream is of fire

to die is to return

NOTES

Epiphany's Prologue

THE GHOSTS OF US – "It is not hard to love a ghost" comes from "Nocturnes & Aubades" (V, A Pact), in *Red Leaves of Night*. New York: HarperCollins, 1999, by David St. John.

"There is such as thing as too much," in X by PB Rippey (as seen in *Crab Creek Review*), unpublished poetry manuscript.

"This is what their bodies are; an opportunity," based on "That's what a body is; an opportunity," from "The Shirley Poem" by Brenda Hillman in *Cascadia*. Wesleyan University Press, 2002.

Water Woman

Reference books used on African proverbs include:
Finnegan, Ruth. *Oral Literature in Africa*. Oxford: Oxford University Press, 1970.
Okphewo, Isidore. *African Oral Literature*. Bloomington: Indiana University Press, 1992.
Courlander, Harold. *A Treasury of African Folklore*. New York: Crown Publishers Inc. 1975.

Fire Woman

LA BREA WOMAN. "To approximate the dimensions of a body." From *To approximate the dimensions of a body hanging from the ceiling from a piece of String* (unpublished MFA manuscript) by Rick Reid.

Stone Woman

STATION IV – "I am this stone in the middle of the road." Inspired by "In the Middle of the Road" by Carlos Drummond de Andrade as translated by Mark Strand in *Looking for Poetry*. New York: Alfred Knopf, 2002.

STATION IV – "It is hard to remain human." From "the times" in *Blessing the Boats*. Lucille Clifton. Rochester, NY: BOA Editions, Ltd., 2000.

STATION XIII – ELEGY. "And the rest is death, and only death", and "And the rest is death, and death alone." From "Lament for Ignacio Sanchez Mejias" in *In Search of Duende* by Frederico García Lorca. New York: New Directions Bibelot, 1955, 1988.

STATION XIII – ELEGY. "If I could match the rage of prophets." From *Fire*, a libretto by Jennifer Kwon Dobbs.

Unholy Woman

DOG WOMAN – The Line – under an open window, a violin – is by Rilke in the *Dueno Elegies*.

MARY – "The gesture, like a fruit torn from a limb, torn swiftly." From "Self Portrait as the Gesture Between Them (Adam and Eve)" in *The End of Beauty* by Jorie Graham. New York: The Ecco Press, 1995.

LUSH – "Necesito . . ." by Pablo Neruda in *Twenty Love Sonnets*.
"that old woman . . . he is guilty of genocide," from "In the Middle of my Life by Taduesz Rozewicz" in *PostWar Polish Poetry: An Anthology Selected* and Edited by Cezlaw Milosz. Berkeley: University of California Press, 1983.

Tree Woman

PRELUDE. "There is a story – I cannot tell it – I have no words," by Sherwood Anderson.

REVELATION. "they're finding bodies everyday now. One clutching grass one the mud." From an untitled as yet unpublished sequence of poems by Rick Reid.

POISON OAK. "Love is apart from all things." From "The Great Fires" in *The Great Fires, poems 1982 - 1992* by Jack Gilbert. New York: Alfred A. Knopf, 2001.

Epiphany's Epilogue

THE POET'S DREAM OF AUTONOMY – "Until no part remains that is surely you." From "Self Portrait in a Convex Mirror" in *Selected Poems*. John Ashberry. New York: Penguin, 1986.

BIOGRAPHICAL NOTE

Chris Abani's novels are *GraceLand* (Farrar, Straus and Giroux, 2004) and *Masters of the Board* (Delta, 1985). His poetry collections include *Daphne's Lot* (Red Hen, 2003), and *Kalakuta Republic* (Saqi, 2001). He teaches in the MFA Program at Antioch University, Los Angeles and is a Visiting Assistant Professor at the University of California, Riverside. A Middleton Fellow at the University of Southern California, he is the recipient of the 2001 PEN USA Freedom-to-Write Award, the 2001 Prince Claus Award and a 2003 Lannan Literary Fellowship.